LIBERAL EDUCATION:

ITS OBJECTS AND METHODS.

An Address at the opening of Bryn Mawr College, U.S.*

As I looked five or six years ago on the unwrinkled face of the founder of this College as he lay in his coffin, with the peace of God upon his brow, I thought of *this* day, and the grief he must have felt when he found he would not live to see it. He had only reached the threescore years and ten of which the Psalmist speaks as an average age of men of health and vigour, and he might reasonably have hoped to add the few more years that would bring him to the opening of the College to which he had given so much thought and so many prayers. The shortness of human life underlies all our enterprises with its inevitable pathos. But as Webster said of States, so may we say of great foundations like this, it is a grand and consolatory reflection that, while men pass away, colleges may be perpetual.

---

* It is proper to state that the address as here printed, in obedience to the request of a few friends, has been modified both by omissions and additions, and that no one is responsible for it but the author. He believes, however, that it contains nothing at variance with the views of the authorities of Bryn Mawr College, which will be found ably stated in the excellent address of President Rhoads at the opening, and the interesting programme prepared by Dean Thomas. The subject of this essay is a very large one, and no pretence is made here of an exhaustive treatment of it. But the views presented are the fruit of long experience and wide observation, and of a sincere desire to find out and proclaim the truth.—T. C.

Even in this world the influence, and in one sense the
life, of JOSEPH WRIGHT TAYLOR shall be perpetuated
to long distant ages in the minds that shall be trained
and the characters that shall be moulded in this
Christian seat of learning.

The feeling deepest in all our hearts at this hour is,
I doubt not, in unison with the desire strongest in the
founder's heart : that the blessing of Him without
whom all our building is in vain may rest upon these
walls, and that the pure, simple, and spiritual truths
of the Gospel of His Son, unmixed with false tradition
and unspoiled by false philosophy, may be taught here
by faithful teachers, received here into willing hearts,
and shown forth in successful lives henceforth and
until the end of time.

The purposes of this College, as announced by your
President, contemplate no narrow or one-sided training.   You aim at whole and complete culture, the
symmetrical development of all the powers that have
been given us, spiritual, mental, and physical.

The most prominent purpose of colleges as it is
generally understood is the culture of the intellect ;
but intellectual vigour itself is promoted by right
and harmoniously-ordered spiritual affections, and is
largely dependent on the health of the body, so that
every college should provide for these ends also so far
as its circumstances permit.   But colleges which,
like Bryn Mawr and Haverford, hold out to their
students, in the years in which personal character
most readily takes on its permanent impression, the
promise of the nurture and training as well as the
comforts of a Christian home, standing *in loco parentis,*
cannot escape the responsibilities of parents for that
spiritual culture which ensures the truest and highest
happiness in this life and in the next, and for the
inculcation of the duty of obeying the laws of bodily
health, so as to have always clear heads, tranquil

LIBERAL EDUCATION:

ITS OBJECTS AND METHODS.

————— ◆●◆ —————

An Address delivered at the opening of Bryn Mawr College, Pennsylvania,

BY

THOMAS CHASE, LL.D. (HARVARD),

*President of Haverford College, U.S.A.; Member of the American Committee
for the Revision of the Translation of the New Testament, &c.*

————— ◆●◆ —————

LONDON.
———
1886.

nerves, steady and vigorous pulses, erect forms, graceful carriage, and general energy, vigour, and self-confidence. This is an ideal higher and broader than any that has been fully attained at the more distinguished colleges and universities of the world ; but if you did not aim at this nobler ideal you would be false to the traditions and aspirations of the religious Society which, through one of its most devoted sons and the agents whom he chose, has built these buildings, assembled these teachers and furnished this endowment, and false to the best thought of the age itself.

The great purposes of college training admit of no narrower definition than this : To fit for life. Lower or higher interpretations may be given to this definition according to one's ideals of success and of the objects of living, but it includes them all so far as they are lawful. To enable a young lady to make an honourable living in any of the professions which are open to her sex, or to make her accomplished, agreeable, and attractive, fitted to shine in any sphere, these are not unworthy objects if associated with an ardent desire to be of some use in the world. But we have higher aspirations and higher ideals of life than pecuniary or social success. The life which we wish to quicken and promote is the life of the whole being, the glad, bright life of the pure and healthy body, the noble, unwearying, ever-expanding life of the mind, the undying life of the intelligent, feeling, willing soul.

I count you happy, the teachers whose privilege it will be to introduce into this large and noble life, and the students who shall here come to know it. For it is a great thing to know : to know thyself, this world into which thou hast come, and the works and laws of nature and of mind,—to know the only true God and Jesus Christ whom He hast sent. And what a charm descends upon these walls, and clothes the rising groves in which they will be embowered, as one thinks of the glad surprises, the thrills of conscious growth and power, that shall bring joy and blessing and unbounded promise for the future to the thousands that will be nurtured in their shade !

A great poet, in words which I hope you all remember, likens his joy at his first introduction into the " pure serene " of Homer's realm, to that of one who discovers a new planet or first looks down upon a new ocean. Such pleasure awaits you, my young friends, and the long line of your successors, as you shall be introduced to the kings of thought and the masters of literature, one after another, of different ages and in many tongues ; or as you study this earth and the universe in which it is placed, learn the structure of its rocks and minerals and soils, and the plants with which it is clothed, and come to know each tree and leaf and blossom, the living creatures which people air and water, field and wood ; and as you discern the facts and laws of chemistry and physics, explore the noble sciences of proportion, form, and number, or rise to the study of man himself—his manners, laws, and institutions, his history, his arts, his languages and literatures, his mind, his moral nature, and his immortal hopes.

In the somewhat chaotic state of opinion in our day in regard to the best courses and plans of study, few deny that a foundation should be laid of general culture, and that afterwards attention should be concentrated upon special fields in which thorough and high proficiency is desired. *What* the foundation should be, is a question to which different answers are given. None would deny that it should include a good knowledge of our own language and skill in speaking and writing it, together with elementary mathematics, geography, and history. Most would add the elements of the physical and natural sciences, and some language or languages other than English. But here the battle begins between the advocates of modern languages alone, and those who favour Greek and Latin as well. I will not attempt, here and now, *tantas componere lites*, but will simply say that there are good educations and good educations, which may differ much and yet be good, each in its own place ; at the same time there is what we may confidently call *the best general education ;* the one best entitled to be called liberal and generous ; and from that best and highest scheme the languages and literatures of Greece and Rome cannot be excluded. I am glad that this fact is recognised in Bryn Mawr College.

No good scheme of education can disregard the importance of disciplinary studies, including classics, mathematics, philosophy, and logic—as distinguished from studies which simply or chiefly present information ; important as the latter undoubtedly are. The studies for information require less time, and can often be pursued as by-play, or left in a measure for one's private reading and research in after life,—for we only *begin* our studies in colleges and universities, —or provided for in special courses for those who wish great proficiency in them. But studies which discipline, develop and strengthen the whole mind, increase its power of concentrating its attention and acting with promptness, vigour, and quick intelligence, and which exercise the faculties of reason and judgment, thus making the mind a more serviceable instrument for any work to which it may be desirable to put it in after years, have an imperative claim for acceptance in all schools and colleges.

In connection with such studies, however, let us have the widest attainable general culture, comprehending the studies which inform as well as those which develop. I use these terms not as exclusive, for disciplinary studies give valuable information, and informing studies, if properly taught, furnish a certain amount of discipline ; nor is it improbable that improved methods of instruction will make the informing studies more and more useful in this way. The liberally educated man may rightly be expected, in addition to his attainments in special fields, to know enough in all the great departments of human knowledge to have some comprehension of the intellectual and scientific life and progress of his age, and to understand at least what people are talking about in any company of scholars and men of science. A man may, it is true, avow his distaste for some classes of studies and his ignorance in them, without forfeiting a high reputation for scholarship or scientific attainments ; but the chief seats of learning should give their students the opportunity of looking into every field, and testing its attractiveness, whether to the rapid tourist or to the life-long explorer.

Among the studies which should be universally required, to a certain extent, a high place belongs to the natural sciences. It is a serious defect in any man's education if he has not at least some elementary knowledge of botany, zoology, mineralogy, geology, and astronomy, enabling him to understand the better and the more fully and keenly to enjoy the objects which surround him in this world. Yet what defect is more common, even among those regarded as the best educated ? With a perfect system of primary and secondary schools, perhaps all the natural history which ought to be required of every student would be learned before coming to college ; for the sciences of observation are especially fit for the earlier years of life. The colleges and universities could then confine themselves to advanced elective courses in these studies. But somewhere this knowledge should be gained. It can be gained, and still time enough be left for ripe and full accomplishment in linguistic and literary studies.

Belonging to the broad school of general culture, I recognise no antagonism between the claims of the natural and physical sciences and those of the mental sciences. But it may be proper for me to speak particularly of some of the latter : the studies which pertain to the mind and its works, and to man and his life upon the earth—such as literature, languages, history, and philosophy.

More wonderful than the crystal, the plant, or the animal, more wonderful than the stars of heaven, is the mind of man, the greatest object which comes within our immediate knowledge in the whole creation. Hence arises the peculiar dignity of all intellectual studies. Wherein is man more fully revealed, wherein does he appear more noble, than in literature and art, philosophy, politics, ethics, and religion ? Wherein can man be so well studied as in these his most characteristic creations and activities ? No one is a warmer advocate than I of the material sciences ; but many examples show that the study of them alone tends easily to blind the eyes to spiritual truths. It has led men of great ability into the error of approaching mental and spiritual phenomena simply from the material side, believing nothing which cannot be seen and analysed in some material fabric, as the brain and nerves, instead of interrogating also thought and consciousness themselves : an error as great as the reverse process of creating the material world out of one's inner consciousness. But he that has studied the masterpieces of literature, or traced the laws of thought and will and feeling, knows that there is in mind itself a power original and great ; never to be explained as the mere product of cerebral chemistry, or neuro-electricity, to whatever extent it may use such agencies as its tools.

The languages of Greece and Rome will never again be considered, as they were once, as almost the sole requisites of a liberal education. The wisest advocates of their study regard them in our day as an extremely valuable instrument, but as only one of many instruments which are needed to work out the best and highest culture. But they have such exquisite perfections, they enshrine such wondrous and delightful creations of genius, and such perfect models of literary art—the springs whence so much flows of what is best in the literatures of modern times ; and they have become so interwoven in the higher life and civilisation of our race, that they will never cease to hold an important place in any scheme of wide and generous education. The mental exercise in the work of translation forms habits of logical analysis, and disciplines the judgment and the faculties of discrimination and choice, affording the best training in the discernment of moral probabilities—probabilities of the same order as those by which our whole practical life is regulated. No studies cultivate more successfully than the classics the habit of patient diligence, without which no eminence can be gained in any department. I need only touch upon the benefit and aid which these studies bring to the memory, the taste, and the imagination ; to the power of exact, forcible, and graceful expression in one's own language, translation being one of the best possible exercises in English composition, and to the vivid conception of the great scenes and the great men of ancient times, besides being themselves (not to speak of the noble writings which they contain of history proper) often the most important of historical documents, or rather one of the most important parts of the history itself of the two great peoples of antiquity—for the study of the literature of any age is historical study of the most intimate sort, penetrating directly to the very thoughts, passions, and inmost personality of the actors.

I need not speak of the value of Latin as a key to

all the Romance languages—a key indispensable to the understanding of their history, the unlocking of their full meaning, and the disclosure of all their treasures. Nor need I remind you that not only are Greek and Roman history best studied in Greek and Latin writers, but that many of the most important documents of mediæval, and sometimes even of modern history, are written in Latin, and that in every art and science known to man, aid is to be derived from treatises in the two classic tongues. And can we not assert the indispensableness of a certain amount of knowledge of Greek and Latin for the highest accomplishment and scholarship, even as a man of science? Shall he be called a master who does not understand the very nomenclature of his own science, and who cannot name his own inventions or discoveries without the aid of a classical scholar?—who cannot, moreover, read the great works of Newton and Leibnitz, and scores of other modern writers, in their originals? The elder Agassiz told me that Aristotle's "History of Animals," in the original Greek, was his constant companion, and that he never read it without wondering at the old philosopher's accuracy of observation and his anticipation of some of the best and boldest generalizations of modern times. I do not mean at all that scientific men ought to be familiar with the minutiæ of elegant classical scholarship; but they should have a general knowledge of the vocabularies and constructions, such as might be acquired by mature and active minds, under skilful instruction, perhaps, through one year's study. I am speaking, too, of scholastic courses, not forgetting how much more genius and industry—as in the case of Franklin and Edison—can do without training, than training alone without genius and industry.

In regard to the Greek, there is one fact which will always give it a valued place in any scheme of high

Christian education, and that is that it is the original
language of the New Testament.   You have all read
enough in other tongues to know that in every great
work of literature in any language there is something
that cannot be adequately and exactly represented in
any other ; some indefinable significance, some fleeting,
nameless charm, some subtle aroma, which vanishes
in translation.   Again, while a version may be correct,
if taken in the sense the translators intended, its words
may be capable of another sense, and one needs the
original in order to understand the version.   There
are sometimes, too, nice distinctions in one language,
—such as that between the verbs φιλέω and ἀγαπάω in
Greek,—which cannot be denoted at all in another
language, unless by long periphrases, which would be
objectionable in a literary point of view.   Consider
also the greater interest and pleasure with which we
read the very words originally used by a sacred writer
or speaker.   On these and many other grounds, the
careful and thorough student of Christianity will regard
a knowledge of the Greek Testament in the original as
indispensable.   The Septuagint version of the Old
Testament has long been recognised as a necessary part
of the apparatus of the Christian scholar, both as an
aid in determining the interpretation and the text
itself of the Old Testament, and from the light it sometimes sheds upon the phraseology and idioms of the
New.   Nor can the student of the history of the Christian Church dispense with an accurate knowledge of
both Greek and Latin, in order to read the Fathers
and the early ecclesiastical historians.

It can be justly demanded, also, of a Christian seat
of advanced learning, that it should provide for instruction in the language of the Old Testament and the
cognate Semitic tongues.

In our immediate vicinity still stands the old colonial
mansion in which the venerable Charles Thomson, the

secretary of the first Continental congress, made his
noble translation of the whole Bible from the Septuagint
version and the Greek New Testament ; a work which
will always be prized and honoured among the monu-
ments of American Biblical scholarship. Who knows
what works in the same field, as creditable to their
times as this was to an earlier day, shall issue from
these walls, or from the kindred shades of Haverford ?

Wise men have feared that the present tendency to
exclusive specialism in university studies will lead to
a lamentable narrowness and onesidedness. This result
has undoubtedly been seen in some cases ; but we may
trust that in time the evil will correct itself. The
man who aims at special excellence will soon find, if
he is far-sighted, that that very purpose will compel
him to make wide excursions in many fields. No one
is likely to understand the modern languages fully,
for example, who does not understand the ancient
languages, from which they are in many cases derived,
and which have in all cases largely moulded their constructions and their canons of taste and style. No one
can understand the ancient languages without being
irresistibly tempted into the attractive neighbouring
fields of the modern tongues. I thought it a very
characteristic as well as delightful thing in the meet-
ings of the American revisers of the translation of the
Greek Testament, that their accomplishment in Greek
was the guarantee of their accomplishment in many
other languages ; so that, when, as often happened
in their discussions, a member cited a passage or an
idiom from another tongue, he read or spoke it in the
original Greek, Latin, Hebrew, German, French, Italian,
or modern Greek, without adding a translation. When
Arabic or Syriac was quoted, a translation was generally given ; but no interpreter was needed by any
one in the other cases, or when Dr. Dorner, of Berlin,
addressed the company for half an hour in German.

Such varied accomplishments, not rare among gentle-
men and scholars,* require in most cases, it is true,
advantages beyond and outside of those offered by colleges and universities, such as foreign travel and years
of private study. In judging the higher schools of
learning themselves we must always bear in mind that
the highest results are reached only when the training of
the college and the university is supplemented by the
devotion of a lifetime. But to return to my propo-
sition, it is no proof of your proficiency in anything
that you know nothing about anything else. Not to
speak of that *commune vinculum* between all studies
which was a commonplace as long ago as the age of
Cicero, no large and active mind can possibly refrain
from pursuing its investigations in many directions,
however wisely it may determine to make some one
thing the chief object of its pursuit. If a great mind
is inevitably many-sided, inferior minds may well cultivate the same quality in due degree. There is rest
and refreshment as well as pleasure in the use of different powers and in occasional wanderings in new
fields ; and it is no small advantage that we are brought
thereby into sympathy with a larger number of our
fellow-men.

It remains true, however, that a man must devote
the larger part of his time to some particular study or
class of studies, after laying a sufficiently broad foundation of general study, if he wishes to make any great
and commanding attainments. This fact, together
with the wide extent of the field of knowledge in our
day, makes " the elective system " a necessity in the
latter years of academic life. The extent of the field
of election, and its divisions and limitations, will be

---

* I may mention the example of a London barrister and his
accomplished family, as one which is familiar to many of my
readers.

determined in part by the size of the college or university, the number of its teachers, and its pecuniary resources.

In view of the liberal provision which has been made here by your generous founder, and of the wise care with which your plans have been made, I congratulate the trustees who have laid broad the foundations of a great seat of literature, art, and science; the accomplished president, who enters upon his most interesting and important work with the full confidence of the community, and with the sure guarantees of success which are offered by Christian faith, large practical wisdom, comprehensive intelligence, steadfast principles, an equable temper, and a firm will; the learned dean and faculty, who bring hither the brightest academic laurels, and engage in a field of congenial labour and high public service; the students, to whom the boon is granted of being the first to drink at these fountains of the muses; our whole community; and the commonwealth of learning itself. I welcome you to the sisterhood of colleges with especial pleasure as a representative of a neighbouring institution of kindred origin and kindred aims.

Allow me to say a few words of cordial welcome to you, the members of my own profession. It is the teachers who mould and control the college or the university. That they should be men and women of ability and great learning, masters in their respective fields, keeping well abreast with all the progress made in their departments in any part of the world, is expected as a matter of course. But knowledge and genius for study are not the only requisites. The successful college teacher must have the power of reading each student's mental character and needs, testing his work, and keeping him up to the proper mark of diligence and faithfulness, and of making him develop to the fullest his own powers by refusing to throw him

scholastic corks and bladders ; and he must also have
the power of laying before him the ripest, richest, most
enticing fruits of knowledge—which he would often
hardly know where to look for himself—as fast as his
mind can assimilate them.   Such a teacher is distinguished by inspiring an ardent interest in the subject
he teaches, and by forming in his pupils the habit of
hard work, which is so essential to happiness and
success : that unflagging and well-directed work which
becomes at length the glad, willing, spontaneous
activity of our noblest powers, the joy of conquest
over difficulties, and a triumphal march through the
fields of learning ; not without dust and heat, but a
dust and heat that we feel not nor regard in the exulta-
tion of victory.

More than this : in the best teachers there is a
potency, an inspiration in the man himself, which
transcends genius and learning, experience, skill, and
tact.   Happy is he who in his youth has been brought
into close communion with the mind and character of
an Agassiz, a Woolsey, a Wayland, or a Mark Hopkins.
Nor is the magic power of deep and wholesome influence confined to great men like these.   Every true
man and true woman can hope to attain to it who
loves youth, and with an earnest heart loves knowledge, truth, and virtue.

Finally, *magnificabo apostolatum nostrum.*   Let us
never forget that we have ends to pursue higher than
the mere imparting of knowledge, even in those great
arts and sciences which we teach.   Let us not forget
that all foundations like this are set to bear a perpetual
testimony to the highest and noblest ideals of life.
They stand as breakwaters against the tide of material
desires and ignoble aims, the love of idle wealth and
sensuous ease, the Circe song.   They point us to the
heights of self-culture, self-knowledge, self-conquest,
self-control, as well as to the shining fields of learning

and science, and the winsome bowers of poetry and art. They reveal—

"A grace of being finer than ourselves;"

they stir us with—

"Intimations clear of wider scope,
Hints of occasion infinite, to keep
The soul alert with noble discontent,
And onward yearnings of unstilled desire."

In the sure hope that this College will do its full part in the fulfilment of this great mission, I hail the promise which this day brings. All hail that long hereafter in which the name of Bryn Mawr shall be a spell to raise or to quicken all noble thoughts and high aspirations, like the names of Bologna and Salamanca, of Paris and Leipzig, of Oxford and Cambridge, of Harvard and Yale!

www.ingramcontent.com/pod-product-compliance
Lightning Source LLC
Chambersburg PA
CBHW082059070426
42452CB00052B/2744